BUSES IN ESSEX
THE 1960S AND 1970S

David Christie

AMBERLEY

Photographed at Clapham
Museum on 12 November
1968 is one of the oldest
Eastern National vehicles to be
preserved – AJN 825, a Bristol
KS5G from 1939. It is shown
here in 'as withdrawn' condition
but in 1974 the bus was restored
to its original red and cream
'Westcliff-on-Sea' livery. It is
now privately owned.

First published 2017

Amberley Publishing
The Hill, Stroud
Gloucestershire, GL5 4EP

www.amberley-books.com

Copyright © David Christie, 2017

The right of David Christie to be identified as
the Author of this work has been asserted in
accordance with the Copyright, Designs and
Patents Act 1988.

ISBN 978 1 4456 7747 7 (print)
ISBN 978 1 4456 7748 4 (ebook)

British Library Cataloguing in Publication Data.
A catalogue record for this book is available from
the British Library.

Origination by Amberley Publishing.
Printed in the UK.

Contents

Introduction

Following on from my book *London Transport Buses in East London and Essex*, which covered the red London Transport (LT) bus routes and Green Line services into Essex, this volume continues the coverage with the LT green Country buses (LC), starting from Epping and Rainham but concentrating mainly on the 370 route from Romford to Tilbury Ferry. This ran from the London Road Green Line garage (RE) forecourt, which was just half a mile from my home and which I passed every day on my way to school/work. Many a time, as a lad, I would board the RT here for a journey from end-to-end of the route, ending up at Tilbury Ferry – a fascinating place with its steam car ferries crossing the Thames to Gravesend. I invariably took the top-deck front seat and recall one memorable return journey from Tilbury at dusk when the driver seemed to prefer driving the country lanes without headlights! RE garage closed with the abandonment of its Green Line services in 1977, by which time I had moved (in 1973) to Scotland. The route joined other services at Grays, which originated from Rainham. The routes in the Grays area had, from 1951 until this point, only been operated by LT, when they were taken over from Eastern National.

The main independent operator in the Hornchurch/Upminster area was Upminster & District, mainly using ex-LT buses, which, apart from their stagecarriage services, were often seen in and around Romford as 'Private'. This company seemed to like ringing the changes through fleet names from 'Super Coaches' to 'City' and 'Blue Line'. Also around Romford at the time were Elm Park Coaches, which operated contract services and used mainly ex-Tilling Group buses in their original liveries. Finally, in the first chapter, a chance encounter with a rare non-standard ex-Cravens-bodied RT run by Red Car, Chigwell, will be seen.

Eastern National buses were familiar as they ran several routes through Romford, but by 1967, when I started photography, they were using fairly modern FLF-type Bristols. These, to my regret, I ignored, being more concerned with capturing the remaining exposed-radiator 'KSW' and single-decker 'LS' types, which were still to be found around Brentwood and out to Southend and Colchester. The company seemed to be unique among the Tilling Group in adopting a policy of silver- (or aluminium-) painted radiators for its vehicles, which to my eyes always gave them a completely different look. I did make an exception to my Lodekka antipathy when I found an early full-depth radiator bus parked in Southend bus station.

Southend's buses – and even trolleybuses – were an early childhood memory through family trips to the seaside, with their very different blue and cream livery. Unfortunately, the trolleys went in 1954 (when I was eleven) but the Southend livery lived on, which always gave an exotic touch when encountered at, say, Rayleigh station, which I used often when visiting my newly married sister and her family. The Corporation tended to do things its own way, sticking with traditional bus types and operating a few of the last exposed-radiator buses built. Another unusual feature was their purchase of ex-Glasgow Royal Tiger single-deckers, which were in operation from 1966 to 1972, and the hire of two similar buses from Bournemouth Corporation in 1970–1, which were operated in their yellow livery. There were also a small fleet of superb ex-Birmingham/Westcliffe/EN Daimlers dating from 1944–5 that were used for their open-top services.

Colchester was a very interesting place for buses when visited in late '67, with its rich brown (officially Tuscan Red) and cream livery and varied small fleet of traditional buses – the most notable, perhaps, being the five Crossleys. Daimlers and AECs were also to be found, as well as several independents operating into the city. Chief of these was Osborne's of Tollesbury, who used exclusively ex-LT types. Their livery was an adaptation of LT and, on the double-deckers, was actually an improvement! Their depot in Tollesbury was a must to visit. H. C. Chambers and Norfolk's were the other independents captured.

The last chapter comprises a few contractors and 'Private' vehicles. It was a case then of not knowing what would be found 'around the corner', sometimes producing some interesting sights; although, with the second-hand market being recently flooded with buses, the real 'gems' were past.

As in my previous book, all images were taken on Agfa CT18 film with a Petri 7 camera until early 1971, when a Minolta SRT101 SLR was used.

David Christie, 2017

London Transport Country
& Independents

Epping station

London Country RF654 arrives at Epping station on 27 March 1970. Early signs of the change in ownership from London Transport to London Country, just two months earlier, are the painting out of the front LT symbol but the LT fleet name remains. The 339 route was worked by both RFs and RTs. RF654 was one of a 700-strong class of AEC Regal IV/Metro-Cammells built in 1951–3.

North Weald

A full LT-liveried RF301 on the 339 route is seen here heading west for Epping and Harlow at North Weald on a sunny 3 January 1970.

Two years on at the same location, RF298 heads in the opposite direction for Brentwood, now in full London Country colours with yellow trim and fleet name. As happened to all LT vehicle types, the rear wheel covers had been removed in late 1971. Photographed on 30 January 1972.

Navestock

RF301 returns from Harlow, heading for Warley at the Navestock road signpost on 3 January 1970.

Brentwood

RT935 leans to the turn out of the High Street, once again on the 339 route, on 16 March 1968. The RT was built from 1947 to 1954 as an AEC Regent III, mainly bodied by Park Royal and Weymann, with a small number by Saunders and Craven. Around 4,600 were built.

Green Line-liveried RT635 is seen at the main High Street stop on route 339. At this time it wasn't uncommon to see ex-Green Line 'coaches' demoted to bus status, and it was always a pleasure to find an LT bus with no adverts. Photographed on 7 June 1969.

A full year later the same vehicle is seen entering the High Street under London Country management with the new fleet name applied and adverts added. Unfortunately, LT's high standards of appearance had taken a nosedive, which is evident here by the body scrapes and an odd-coloured front offside wing. Photographed on 13 June 1970.

RT635 again, in its original Green Line colours, seen in the High Street on 7 June 1969.

RT3606 turns into the High Street from Station Road on route 339, on 13 June 1970.

A last look at ex-Green Line RT635, pulling uphill from Brentwood station on 13 June 1970. Route 339 kept its RTs until 1976, when they were replaced by hired Southend Corporation PD3s.

Romford London Road Garage Forecourt

The terminus of the 370 route, London Road Green Line garage (coded RE) forecourt is seen here with two RTs – 4114 and 3153 – on 30 July 1968. One is showing a short working to Chadwell.

RT3153 now leaves the forecourt on its journey to Tilbury Ferry. As described in the Introduction, the 370 was a favourite ride.

RE garage forecourt on 13 June 1970 shows both the old and the new order. RT4733 has been joined by RMC1515, which was demoted from Green Line work on the 723 routes operated by Grays garage. On the building to the right of the buses, the large 'London Transport' letters have been removed. Both buses unusually show short Grays destinations. The RMC class was the coach version of the Routemaster bus, with sixty-eight being built in 1962.

RT3462 is seen about to turn into the RE garage forecourt on 17 October 1970, with the autumn trees of Cottons Park and the 'new' brewery chimney showing well. The RT's blind setting is a sign of the times, as is the blanking out of the LT triangular radiator plate.

Back to pure LT on a snowy 8 February 1969 with RT3889 setting off for Tilbury.

RT3510 arrives at the end of its cold journey.

RT3601 turns into RE forecourt with the conductor giving the left turn signal. The use of large route numbers on the rear blind was becoming more commonplace. London Country's new emblem adorns the garage entrance.

Romford Centre Traffic Lights

RT4476 turns from South Street into High Street at the Golden Lion public house crossroads, with half a mile to travel to its terminal lay-up at RE garage. This crossroads was the centre of the town until a ring road was built. Construction of this started in 1968 but was completed in several stages, with traffic still using South Street and High Street at the date this photograph was taken, 18 May 1970.

Romford Station

RMC1475 passes under the station bridge in South Street on 8 May 1974, it being two years since RTs operated on the 370. The cantrail relief band between decks is now in LC's yellow.

Romford South Street

Beyond the station, ex-Green Line RT3438 promotes the 'Green Rover' at a cost of seven shillings (35 new pence). Photographed on 8 December 1969.

Further along the street, RT3193 in 'normal' full LT trim passes a cyclist on 17 July 1967.

Romford Roneo Corner

By 1972 ex-Green-Line RCLs were to be found on the 370 route in addition to the RMCs. RCL2240 has lost its original details, such as window contrast edging, radiator badge and rear wheel covers, but still retains its Green Line fleet name and light green cantrail, albeit now with a side advert displayed. The bus still looks fairly smart – if only the rear wheel covers were still present. The RCLs were a lengthened version of the RMC, built in 1965 with most of the forty-three-strong class being used from RE garage on the 721 route. These were the ultimate Routemaster, but were displaced by single-deck coaches after only seven years, with the 721 route having lost custom. It would be abandoned altogether in 1977. Photographed on 15 April 1972.

Hornchurch Church
RT4192 passes the church on 3 February 1970.

Hornchurch RD Garage

The 'Green Rover' RT3438 passes the garage on 3 June 1970. A red RT pokes its nose out of the garage while a Ford Classic pulls away from Lens' Hairdressers.

Hornchurch White Hart

RT4192 passes some fine old buildings near the White Hart on 29 May 1967.

Hornchurch Harrow Lodge Park

RT3656 is seen in sunshine and showers on 21 May 1970 with another odd blind showing.

Corbets Tey

The 370 route had now reached more rural surroundings near Corbets Tey, with RT3189 on 1 November 1969.

RT3241 passes the Huntsman & Hounds pub on 27 March 1968.

North Stifford

RT3498 climbs the steep hill here on 6 April 1968. It seems a rover ticket cost a shilling less then.

RT3889 is seen by the river bridge on 12 April 1971.

Rainham

The 370 route is now left, north of Grays, where routes from Rainham converge. Reversing as it were westwards to Rainham terminus, RTs on route 328 as well as RFs on the 371 routes were to be found. RF545 with RTs 3251 and 3153 are at the church stop on 25 June 1970.

RF33 on the 371B route arrives as a Vauxhall Victor estate extricates itself from between RT4481 and RF545. An RT conductor complete with Gibson ticket machine is seen in this view of 25 June 1970.

RT4144 passes 'Modified' RF64 at the church on 25 June 1970. The Modified RFs were rebuilt in 1967 with twin headlights, a curved windscreen and fluorescent lighting. They were also given a smart two-tone livery with a broad (being Green Line) pale green band, which, on demotion to LC bus work, became yellow, as here.

RT4481 turns on the 328, passing a red RT on route 87. Routemaster blinds appear to have been used at the rear, with destination left blank. Photographed 25 June 1970.

RT4481 is now seen turned, with another vacant blind at the front.

Aveley Usk Road

The full London Country livery is displayed by RT3051 arriving at the terminus on 27 March 1971. This was one of the RTs refurbished by LT at their Aldenham works – and they had made a superb job of it.

RT3051 turns at the terminus.

A nearside view of RT3051, which turned at Aveley.

West Thurrock
RF116, on route 374, passes the cement works on 6 April 1968. The standard LT bus stop full display of all routes passing is well shown.

RT4506 in 'hybrid' livery on route 300 by the cement works on 25 February 1972. This route would change to RM operation just two months later.

RF233 seen in full LC trim passes on the 374, also photographed on 25 February 1972.

North Grays

We are now back where we left off, following the 370 route – with RT3890 on 6 April 1968. My 'fastback' Hillman Imp has also been captured by the camera at less than a year old.

RT4767 on route 328 heads into Grays – also on 6 April 1968.

Green Line-liveried RT650 is employed on bus route 328, leaving Grays on 6 April 1968.

Three years later, with identical route blinds but on a 'standard' RT with adverts, RT3189 leaves Grays on 27 March 1971.

RF33 follows the RT on the 323 route out of Grays. The painted-over LT symbol on the front certainly seemed an amateurish way of changing identities.

Grays Centre

RT3601 looking rather odd without its offside advert panel in traffic in the town centre on the 370. The LC symbol has been applied to the rear offside. Photographed on 27 March 1971.

RT4192 on the 328 route with an odd mixture of blinds, no front adverts and yellow cantrail but still managing to look smart. A small point, but the black painted-out radiator triangle looks much better than the more usual green. Photographed on 27 March 1971.

RT3447 on a short 370 working is seen on a quiet Easter Monday, 12 April 1971.

RF243 takes on a rather alarming lean as it turns by the war memorial on route 371. This RF had managed to hang on to its cream-bordered LT symbol despite being under LC management for over a year. Photographed on 12 April 1971.

RT3241, one of the batch of Green Line RTs that worked the 721 route until 1965, now working from Grays garage on the rather minimal-information 328, leaves the daffodils behind at the war memorial on 12 April 1971.

Near Grays

An unidentified RT on a (just) identifiable 370 route crosses the road on 27 March 1971. It seems London Country were not having any of London Transport's route information nonsense!

An unusual view of ex-Green Line RCL2234 on the 328 route dated 25 February 1972. The untidy painting over of the Green Line fleet name and odd (primer?) coloured cantrail could be explained by the vehicle just having been demoted from 721 Green Line service. It has also escaped the November 1971 edict that all rear wheel discs be removed – but perhaps it took longer to take effect out 'in the sticks'!

Grays Garage

RF243, complete with LT emblem, poses outside Grays garage with blinds set for the 371A on 12 April 1971. RTs are visible inside the garage.

RF217, with a long line of RTs in various Country and ex-Green Line liveries at the garage on 10 October 1971. This RF was the only one I had come across bearing the LC symbol on its front.

The very different look at Grays on 11 February 1973 with a complete array of Routemasters – both RMCs and RCLs. How tightly packed these buses were fascinated me!

Tilbury

Another RF retaining the LT symbol – RF690 on route 371A – leaves a housing estate at Tilbury on 27 March 1971. This retention of the old management emblem (with only the LT words painted out) seemed to be a feature of Grays-garaged RFs.

RT4725 crosses the railway line on the new bridge not far from the ferry terminus of the 370. Photographed on 27 March 1971.

Tilbury Ferry

On a lovely evening, ex-GL RT3635 arrives at the ferry terminus on 27 March 1971.

RT3635 comes alongside Eastern National 2756, a Bristol FLF/ECW (built 1962) on EN route 155.

RT3635 reverses with the help of the conductress on 27 March 1971. The last RTs worked on the 370 in March 1972.

London Country RMC1475 arrives at the ferry on 25 February 1972. A dark blue BR (ER) 'Way Out' sign is also captured.

Upminster & District – Romord Western Road

KYY 503 was the only Upminster & District bus seen in their light blue livery, with the curved fleet name. It was also the only ex-LT RLH type I ever saw in Romford, being ex-RLH 3, a 1950 AEC Regent III/ Weymann lowbridge, while some of the later 1952 batch were still to be found working the LT 248 route 'up the road' in Upminster. KYY503 was later sold to an American buyer. Photographed on 29 May 1967.

Upminster & District – Romford Heath Park Road

LYR 918, unusually, came third-hand to the company, originally as LT RT3499, before moving to Ledgards, Leeds, until its purchase by Upminster & District in late 1967. The roof route number box has been removed, and the destination display reduced. It is seen here at Heath Park Road roundabout on 27 March 1969.

Upminster & District – Romford Burnthouse Corner

LLU 916 was ex-LT RTL926, one of the Metro-Cammell-bodied batch that were immediately recognisable from the 'standard' RT/RTL body by the narrower between-decks cantrail. It had been fitted with a platform door and also had its front destination display altered. The late evening sun catches the bus on 28 March 1969.

Upminster & District – Hornchurch Elmhurst Drive

An unusual type in the predominantly ex-LT fleet was FJN 204, a 1952-built Leyland PD2/12 with Leyland body for Eastern National – originally at Westcliff-on-Sea. An odd feature was the rear wheel discs, which were rarely seen outwith LT. Photographed on 5 March 1968.

Upminster & District – Hornchurch

LUC 333 is another Metro-Cammell RTL (958), but this one is seen with original features. It was photographed by the church on 26 March 1968.

Upminster & District – Upminster Bridge Depot

MXX 39 turns into the depot at Upminster Bridge on 27 March 1968. This had been LT RT2951, which had been fitted with an early body before sale by LT – the deeper cantrail over the engine compartment identifies it. It has, however, lost its roof route number box.

City – Romford Burnthouse Corner

The 'City' livery adopted by Upminster & District from 1970 was a reincarnation of that used by the City Coach Co., which most famously ran the London Wood Green to Southend service up until 1952 and used twin front-axled Leyland Gnus – at times creating havoc when turning from North Street into Market Place, Romford. LUC 19 (ex-LT RT1939), which is pictured here, however, is not so exotic but looks splendid in its new livery (despite its Saunders body having a broken glass top box. Most unusually it sports a full LT triangular badge on its radiator. It had just been purchased when photographed on 8 June 1970.

City – Upminster Station

Another Saunders-bodied bus, KLB 773 (ex-LT RT2394), runs a schools service on 30 May 1970. The otherwise smart look (now with 'City' name) is spoilt by the tatty side advert.

City – Upminster Bridge Depot
KLB 773 again, seen about to run under the railway bridge before turning into the Upminster & District depot on 4 June 1970.

City – Romford Waterloo Road

A rear view of LYR 904 (ex-LT RT3485) about to pass under the railway bridge in Waterloo Road on 17 October 1970. Romford Brewery buildings are visible beyond.

City – Hornchurch 'Optimist' Terminus

KLB 762 (ex-LT RT2383) at the Optimist pub terminus on 27 March 1971. The otherwise attractive livery is ruined by the appalling state of its adverts – it appears that the paint job had been applied *around* the adverts, with LT red showing through! The company seemed to have a policy of only using their buses for two years, invariably withdrawing them for sale or scrap, so perhaps that's why they did not take more care of their appearance.

Blue Line – Upminster Bridge Depot

This shows the last (as far as I was concerned) transformation that Upminster & District buses went through. The fleet name was now 'Blue Line', with a rather odd shade of blue. Turning into the depot on 25 January 1972 is KGU 46 (ex-LT RTL596).

KLB 659 (ex-LT RT1571) with an 'intact' Saunders body runs under the railway bridge after leaving the depot on 25 January 1972.

Elm Park Coaches – Romford North Street

Elm Park were a small company operating out of Oldchurch Road, Romford. They tended not to repaint their buses but an exception was this ex-LT RT 2747 (LYR 731). It was found in a temporary car park in North Street on 20 July 1967.

Elm Park Coaches – Gidea Park Main Road

Ex-Thames Valley FMO 946, a 1950 Bristol LL/ECW still in original colours, is seen on 3 April 1968.

Elm Park Coaches – Mawney Road

HMO 867 is also an ex-Thames Valley Bristol (an LS from 1955), and is seen here passing Mawney Road School on 3 March 1970.

Red Car Hire Service, Chigwell

A rare sight in the Romford area was an ex-London Cravens-bodied RT. This is the only one ever seen in Essex, at Marks Gate roundabout on 1 May 1969, bearing the 'Red Car Hire Service' name. KGK 721 (ex-RT1462) shows its body detail differences to the standard RT, with five instead of four side windows (lower deck) and a squarer, upright front profile (although the rooftop route box had been removed).

The rear view of Red Car's KGK 721 shows the more rounded back end; essentially it was a normal Craven body modified to look like a standard RT.

Eastern National

North of Brentwood
On its way to Blackmore is Bristol LS5G/ECW 1237, from 1956. Photographed on 10 May 1974.

Brentwood
KSW5G/ECW 2363 from 1953 is seen at the High Street stop on route 253. This bus had just one year left in service. Photographed on 7 June 1969.

KSW5G 2373 (1953) pulls away from the stop in the High Street on 13 June 1970. The 'via' route boxes appear to be abandoned and painted green. 2373 was withdrawn in October 1970.

LS5G 1240 (1956) on route 250 by the White Hart pub, seen on 13 June 1970.

Another LS 5G, 1231 (1955), turns at the Kings Road traffic lights on route 260, heading to the depot on 13 June 1970. A schoolboy complete with cap looks on.

KSW5G 2363 (1953) heads north away from the main crossroads on route 265. It is fitted with platform doors. Photographed on 7 June 1969.

Brentwood Depot

Three KSW5Gs lined up at the depot on 16 March 1968: 2363, 2337 and 2362. These buses had a variation in withdrawal dates, the earliest, 2337, being withdrawn in July 1968 and 2363 in 1970, with 2362 lasting until February 1971.

LS5G 1235 (1956) turns from the depot road to take up route 261 on 13 June 1970.

Brentwood

LS5G 1231 (1955) heads for Coxtie Green, just 1½ miles from Brentwood, on route 260. Photographed on 13 June 1970.

KSW5G 2373 (1953) on the 253 route heads for the station on 6 June 1970. This bus was withdrawn in October 1970.

Halfway-House Roundabout A12, West Horndon
KSW5G 2337 (1952) on route 265 heads for Brentwood. Photographed on 23 May 1967.

Rayleigh Weir

KSW5G 2374 (1953) on route 25A heads for Thorpe Bay on 23 April 1968. This bus was withdrawn in October 1970.

Rayleigh Station

A very rare (for me) shot of a Lodekka type, probably as it was posed with a traditional Leyland! Unfortunately, I concentrated on the remaining KSWs at the time – a cause for regret now. Here is LD5G 2433 (1956) alongside Southend-on-Sea Corporation Leyland PD3/6 with Massey 338 body, which was built in 1965. Photograph taken on 26 July 1969.

Thundersley

Back to KSWs, and ex-Daws Heath 2344 (1952) on route 25A is pictured on 2 April 1968. This bus was withdrawn in April 1969.

Southend Victoria Station

Taken at the new roundabout that threatened to engulf Victoria station, KSW 2377 (1953) is about to disappear beneath me on route 25 on 10 October 1968. This bus was in service for another two years. Intriguingly, 'Romford' appears (just) at the bottom of the 'via' blind, but the KSW type had ceased to run to my home town by the time that I had started photography.

Southend Bus Station

LS5G 1232 (1955) leaves the bus station on route 12 for Wallasea Bay, passing some old trolleybus standards still in use for street lighting. The trolley system closed in 1954. Photograph taken on 12 April 1971.

Another personally rare shot of Lodekkas, but the far bus with the full-depth radiator clinched the shot for me! Here are three different Lodekka variations together, starting with the far bus, a 1954 LD6B. The radiator style changed with later-built models such as 2431, from 1956, which was another LD6B. The nearest bus shown is 2538, an FS5G from 1960, which shows various detail differences in appearance from the LD. Photographed on 10 October 1971.

Southend Pier

One of the open-toppers converted from a standard KSW (2383, dating from 1953) runs under Southend Pier Bridge on 26 July 1969.

Colchester
1952-built KSW5G 2328 arrives in Colchester on route 76. This bus was withdrawn in July 1968. Photograph taken 1 July 1967.

Just another KSW? No, it's a KS5G – the big difference being that it is 7 feet 6 inches wide as opposed to a KSW's 8 feet. Note the driver's steering wheel is black, whereas all 8-foot-wide models had white steering wheels. 2306, built in 1950, was one of only seven KS types operated by EN and was withdrawn by the end of 1967; this picture was taken on 1 July 1967, so I just made it in time. I had, however, completely missed seeing any remaining 'K' types – I had to go south, to Hampshire and Dorset, to see these still running in 1969!

Ixworth (Suffolk)

Not photographed in Essex, but an Essex bus with a giveaway registration. ONO 87 was ex-Eastern National 195, which was a 1949 Bedford OB. It was one of a twenty-two-strong class, most of which were still with EN in 1959 but did not figure in their 1962 lists. This example, showing 'Robby's Coaches', was found at Mulleys depot at Ixworth, Suffolk, on 11 October 1969.

3

Southend-on-Sea Corporation

Near Victoria Station

A Leyland PD2/12 with Massey 296 body, built in 1955, is seen near Victoria station on route 7. It was one of twelve of this type, which lasted until 1971. Pictured on 13 April 1968, this shot was the only one taken to show the older style of livery with the full 'Southend Corporation Transport' title in the cream area below the lower deck windows and a mainly blue roof.

Pier Hill

317, an AEC Bridgemaster with a Park Royal body (one of only six) from 1959 climbs the hill, passing Leyland PD2/12 with Massey 287 body (1955) descending, both of which are in a more simplified livery. Unlike its classmate shown on the previous page, 287 has non-opening front top windows (but both classes were similarly withdrawn by 1972). Photographed on 10 October 1968.

Rayleigh Weir

Parked in the Rayleigh Weir pub's car park on 23 April 1968 is one of the six-strong class of AEC Regent IIIs with Massey bodies, dating from 1950 and withdrawn in 1965. Although showing the registration EHJ 443, making it 259, it transpired that this bus was actually 261, which should have the registration EHJ 445. What happened was that it had acquired the radiator, complete with affixed registration plate, from the other bus, which was being scrapped. It has been fitted with platform doors and was undergoing preparation for a world tour.

Southend Depot

Parked within the depot in use as a general store is 270, a Daimler CWA6, the chassis of which dated from 1945. This bus was ex-London Transport, and was fitted with a new Massey body when purchased from LT in 1954. It survived until 1979, when it was used to provide parts for sister bus 263's preservation. The large old-style fleet number is prominent. Photographed on 14 March 1971.

Town Centre

Turning into the main street is 307, a 1957-built Leyland PD2/40 with Massey body (one of six). The simplified livery is more evident in this photograph, which was taken on 10 October 1968. This bus was withdrawn in 1971.

316, a Leyland PD3/6 with Massey body, new in 1958, is from the next batch of six. These were the first 30-footers operated. Four of these were rebuilt in 1971 to open-top to take over from the pre-war Daimlers. The rebuilds lasted until 1980, whereas the two remaining went in 1978. Photographed on 12 April 1971.

Central Station

Five of these 1956-built Leyland Royal Tiger 'Worldmaster'/Weymann single-deckers were purchased from Glasgow Corporation in 1966 and worked until 1972. Here is 210 at Central station on 14 March 1971.

Sister bus 213 leaves Central station on 12 April 1971. The two differing livery applications (and destination indicators) on the Eastern National FLFs make interesting comparisons.

Priory Park

From November 1970 to June 1971 two single-deckers were hired from Bournemouth Corporation, providing a splash of yellow amid the blue and cream. These were 1953-built Leyland PSU1/13 with Burlingham-bodied buses, of which 89 is seen here passing Priory Park on 19 March 1971.

Near Central Station

Hired Bournemouth 89 in the main street near Central station on 12 April 1971.

Kursaal

Southend's open-top fleet of four vintage buses originated as 1944–5 Utility Daimler CWA6s that were purchased from Birmingham Corporation in 1955–6, at which point they were rebuilt to open-top. This was re-done in 1963 to show the condition photographed here on 6 July 1968 – this one being 245.

Leigh
245 leaves the Leigh terminus on 6 July 1968.

Seafront
245, in its last year of operation, runs along the seafront on 6 June 1970. Even in their last season they were kept in immaculate condition. One of the batch survived to preservation.

Leigh

245 climbs up from the seafront at Leigh on 6 June 1970.

245 is seen once again at Leigh. All four Daimlers were replaced for 1971 by 1958-built Leyland PD3s.

Pier Hill
316, seen earlier in the town centre, is about to descend to the pier on 12 April 1971.

The pier roundabout with PD3 315 on a busy Easter Monday, 12 April 1971.

315 now climbing Pier Hill.

Sister bus 316, passing 346, was one of three Leyland PD3/4s with East Lancs bodies from 1968, which were among the last exposed-radiator types made.

Kursaal

PD3/4 315 from 1968 at the Kursaal on 12 April 1971. The upright style of the East Lancs body was a real contrast from the curvaceous Massey products favoured over the years. These PD3s had the distinction of being hired by London Country for nine months in 1976. They had all been withdrawn by 1981.

4

Colchester Corporation & Independents

City Centre

One of four all-Crossley DD42/7 buses dating from 1951–2 is seen in the city centre. Making an attractive sight in its 'Tuscan Red' livery is Crossley 8 (1952), which was photographed on 1 July 1967. All four Crossleys were withdrawn from April to June 1968.

Crossley 7 (1951) carried a revised version of the livery with much more cream – but balanced by the red (brown) strip under the top deck windows. The headlamps were set higher than on 8, which looked better. Crossley 7 climbs into the city centre on 1 July 1967.

Housing Estate

Crossley 7 again, at its terminus at a housing estate, on 9 September 1967. The predominantly cream livery shows well in this shot – especially the 'Colchester Corporation' fleet name given prominence within a cream band below the lower deck windows. All in all, a brilliant blend of traditional and modern!

City Centre
Really traditional were the five-strong class of Daimler CVD6 with Roberts bodies. Here is 3 dating from 1949, passing a church in the city on 1 July 1967. The painted surround radiator is unusual for this operator. As with the Crossleys, they were all withdrawn in 1968.

Bus Station

Daimler 5 seen arriving at the bus station on 7 September 1967. This bus has a chromed surround radiator, and also rather mismatched headlamps.

Just three AEC Regent IIIs dating from 1953 with Massey bodies were operated. Here is 10 arriving at the bus station on 7 September 1967. These Regents lasted until 1971.

Station Stop

Regent 12 is seen here near the station on 7 September 1967. The large, shaded fleet numbers seemed to be unique to this class.

City Centre

This Crossley, 55, a DD42/3 model from 1948, bodied by Massey, was a 'one-off' in the fleet. This bus had, probably, the worst mismatching headlamps of all, but they seemed to be a feature of most of the fleet. Photographed on 7 September 1967, this bus was withdrawn on 29 September.

Crossley 9 (needing a new mudguard) threads through the gap between buildings on the late afternoon of 9 September 1967.

Barracks Road

Crossley 9, pictured in Barracks Road on 9 September 1967.

North Hill

Crossley 7 climbs North Hill on 9 September 1967.

Osborne's – Colchester

Osborne's of Tollesbury ran a bus fleet of (at the time) 100 per cent ex-London Transport vehicles in various adaptations of LT livery. Running into Colchester on 1 July 1967 is their 26 (ex-LT RF257), which was purchased from LT in January 1965 and withdrawn in May 1971.

Osborne's – Tollesbury Depot

A visit to Osborne's depot on 8 March 1969 produced an interesting line-up of three RFs, with 37 (ex-RF264) being sandwiched between 19 (ex-RF5) and 20 (ex-RF10). The two lower numbered RFs were from the first batch of RFs, which were private hire coaches in a shorter length with glass roof panels for sightseeing. Osborne's painted these in a three-tone livery, with the upper parts contrasting very much as LT had done when the buses built, although LT's colours were a more subdued green and grey. 37 was bought from LT in 1965 and the two earlier RFs in 1964, and all were withdrawn by the end of 1969.

21 (ex-LT RT3671) is looking smart despite the oil filler spill. The three black-edged cream bands were a really simple 'improvement' on the LT livery. 21 was bought in 1964 and was withdrawn in 1971.

Parked inside the garage building is 29 (ex-LT RTW256) – an unusual type to come across operating for an independent. Purchased in 1966, by 1974 it was sold to a dealer after use as a caravan.

Osborne's – Tollesbury Village

RF24 arrives at the village. This bus is ex-LT RF147, which was bought in late 1964 and withdrawn in 1970. Note the round replacement trafficators. All photographs at Tollesbury were taken on 8 March 1969.

21 (ex-RT3671) arrives in Tollesbury village. The round blinkers (as on RF24) stand out here.

Osborne's – Tollesbury Village Square

The village square with red RF24 having arrived, and 'short' 20 waiting to leave for Witham.

Next to arrive at the square is 39 (ex-RT2827) on the Maldon service. This RT has been given platform doors.

39 now picks up passengers at the square. This bus still survives under preservation in Osborne's colours at the Castle Point Transport Museum in Canvey Island.

39 under way – captured just around the corner of the road where my car was parked.

Osborne's – Near Chelmsford
RTW 29 found parked near Chelmsford, along with two RTs on 7 June 1969.

H. C. Chambers & Son – Colchester
Ex-Red & White HWO 341, a 1949 Guy Arab III with Duple body, arrives in Colchester on 1 July 1967.

H. C. Chambers & Son – Colchester Bus Station
Arriving at the bus station on 7 September 1967 is KCF 711, a 1956 Guy Arab IV/Roe that was, unusually for an independent, purchased new in 1956.

Norfolk's – Colchester

Norfolk's TWL 928, ex-City of Oxford 1953 AEC Regent III with Park Royal body, arrives at Colchester on 1 July 1967 looking very well kept and without the usual dents and bashes found in second-hand vehicles. Norfolk's kept this bus running until February 1972 and it is now to be found restored to its Oxford livery at the Oxford Bus Museum at Long Hanborough.

Cedric Coaches (Wivenhoe) – Near Colchester

Parked in a car park near Colchester on 8 March 1969 is MPH 645, a 1948 AEC Regal III/Harrington new to Surrey Motors, Sutton.

5

Contractors & Private

Kilpatrick – Tilbury

Parked near Tilbury Ferry on 13 May 1967 are ex-Paisley & District XS 5723 (a 1946 Guy Arab II/NCME Utility) and ex-Devon General ETT995 (a 1953 Saunders/Roe-bodied 1937 AEC Regent/Regal units combination). Both are a long way from home!

At the same spot on 6 April 1968, GRY 735 is a 1950 Dennis Lancet III/Yeates coach that was new to Clayton, Leicester.

Another full-fronted coach nearby is LAL 799, a 1950 Leyland PS2/3 with a Burlingham body that was new to Robin Hood, Nottingham. It later moved to Blackwell, Sible Hedingham, Essex – a local connection.

Wiggins Thundersley

MPU 24 is an ex-Eastern National 1947 Bristol K5G/ECW, which is seen here by the shops at Thundersley on the evening of 26 March 1968.

At Wiggins depot in Thundersley is DDR 414, a 1947 all-Leyland PD1 ex-Plymouth Corporation bus. In 1970 it was purchased for preservation and returned to its former territory. Pictured on 11 July 1967.

Ex-Portsmouth Corporation – Romford

Parked in a temporary car park by Coronation Gardens, Romford, is ex-Portsmouth Corporation GTP 978, a 1952 all-Leyland PD2/10 that went out of service in 1969. Still in its original livery, I suspect that it may have become a contract bus for Upminster & District. Photographed on 6 March 1970.

Fords, Warley

OLD 845 (ex-LT RTL1616) is seen parked at Fords Offices at Warley on 20 September 1969.

Phoenix, Pitsea – Romford
GDL 434 caught on Eastern Avenue, Romford on 29 May 1967 is a 1950 Bristol K5G /ECW ex-Southern Vectis.

Private

At Havering village on 3 January 1970 was GFN 261, a Leyland/Beadle semi-chassisless coach with TD5 components that was new to East Kent Road Car Co. in 1952.

Squirrels Heath Scouts – Romford

In the Squirrels Head PH Car Park on 8 April 1969 was 1949 BedfordOB/Duple LBH 107, which was owned at the time by Squirrels Heath Scouts (although it was originally owned by Lucasian Coaches, Buckinghamshire). The Scouts certainly kept it in great condition.

Canvey Sea Anglers Club – Romford

One of the delights in those days was coming across a gem such as this Dennis Lancet coach, which dated from the late 1940s/early 1950s. DHM 768, a London registration, was parked in St Andrews Road, Romford, close to the LT London Road garage, on 23 September 1967.